IF NOT FOR YOU

"If it had not been the Lord who was on our side — let Israel now say — if it had not been the Lord who was on our side when people rose up against us, then they would have swallowed us up alive, when their anger was kindled against us; then the flood would have swept us away, the torrent would have gone over us; then over us would have gone the raging waters. Blessed be the Lord, who has not given us as prey to their teeth! We have escaped like a bird from the snare of the fowlers; the snare is broken, and we have escaped! Our help is in the name of the Lord, who made heaven and earth."

PSALM 124:1–8 ESV

Why the Psalms?

This book is a collection of Psalms curated by the author not to be comprehensive but to be collectively inspiring excerpts from the book as a whole to challenge and inspire the reader to dive more deeply into the rest of the Psalms.

We live in an era where we sing the "hymns of old" and recite songs from a time before us as a part of our beloved history of worship to our God. Finding the connection of a heart penning worship, praise and pain - desperation and deliverance - even though they were in an ancient time, connects us all to the need we have for God that neither time nor space can shift. I wonder if you have ever thought about the Psalms as a part of this collection of "hymns of old." They are the ancient praises, adorations, cries, and songs of writers worshipping the one true God. They are the language from which our worship and adoration has continued in melody and song throughout the centuries and they are a place to begin again today to reset our eyes and hearts on our God.

PSALM
91

"He who dwells in the shelter of the Most High will abide in the shadow of the Almighty. I will say to the Lord, "My refuge and my fortress, my God, in whom I trust." For he will deliver you from the snare of the fowler and from the deadly pestilence. He will cover you with his pinions, and under his wings you will find refuge; his faithfulness is a shield and buckler. You will not fear the terror of the night, nor the arrow that flies by day, nor the pestilence that stalks in darkness, nor the destruction that wastes at noonday. A thousand may fall at your side, ten thousand at your right hand, but it will not come near you. You will only look with your eyes and see the recompense of the wicked. Because you have made the Lord your dwelling place— the Most High, who is my refuge— no evil shall be allowed to befall you, no plague come near your tent. For he will command his angels concerning you to guard you in all your ways. On their hands they will bear you up, lest you strike your foot against a stone. You will tread on the lion and the adder; the young lion and the serpent you will trample underfoot. "Because he holds fast to me in love, I will deliver him; I will protect him, because he knows my name. When he calls to me, I will answer him; I will be with him in trouble; I will rescue him and honor him. With long life I will satisfy him and show him my salvation."

Psalm 91 ESV

ONE

"He who dwells in the shelter of the Most High will abide in the shadow of the Almighty. I will say to the Lord, "My refuge and my fortress, my God, in whom I trust."

Psalm 91:1-2 ESV

We begin this devotional together with this phrase, "If not for you." I wonder what chord that strikes for you as you let it play through your mind, write it on paper or maybe say it aloud right now. If not for you, God. If not for you, where would I be? If not for your mercy, grace, and compassion over my life; if not for your rescue and salvation of the earth; if not for your kindness; if not for your sovereignty: where would I be? The wonder this stirs for us is undeniable, when we truly take in the magnitude of what this life would be without our Savior. Maybe you remember a time when you navigated your life apart from Him and it is a contrast that throws you to your knees in gratitude.
In the story Hannah Hurnard so beautifully penned, "Hinds' Feet On High Places," we read the journey of Much Afraid traveling to the high places with the Shepherd. The story comes from Habakkuk 3:19 (ESV), "God, the Lord, is my strength; he makes my feet like the deer's; he makes me tread on my high places. To the choirmaster: with stringed instruments." It is an allegory of the Christian devotional life from salvation to maturity. We see her begin in the valley of Humiliation and end her journey in the High Places, trusting as the Shepherd equips and trains her for each new part of the journey. If not for the Shepherd, she would have never left the Valley to travel to the High Places.

It is the nature of this God-life to grow season by season navigating each new challenge with Him by our side. It is in this journey that we learn to hear the whispers of the Holy Spirit, our guide. In these foothills, valleys, and ascensions of mountain paths, we learn to follow the roadmap of God's word and trust the faithfulness of our Father in heaven. These moments are where we believe and know like never before that He is faithful. He is like a northern star, showing us the way to His heart and the shadow of

His wings. He never leaves or forsakes us. We grow as we journey onward in this pilgrimage, each of our experiences building on each other. They are memorial stones. Each one a marker of roads traveled and trust learned with the Messiah.

"If not for you, God. If not for you, where would I be?"

Open your bible to Psalm 91. We will spend each week reading this Psalm, writing it, and committing it to memory. As Psalm 119:11 tells us, "I have stored up your word in my heart, that I might not sin against you." We are going to store up this Psalm in our hearts as we meditate on it together. I pray that this scripture becomes a memorial marker of these days spent seeking God together. I pray you recall it for decades to come, retelling stories of God's faithfulness in these times to generation upon generation.

"He who dwells in the shelter of the Most High will abide in the shadow of the Almighty. I will say to the Lord, "My refuge and my fortress, my God, in whom I trust." For he will deliver you from the snare of the fowler and from the deadly pestilence. He will cover you with his pinions, and under his wings you will find refuge; his faithfulness is a shield and buckler. You will not fear the terror of the night, nor the arrow that flies by day, nor the pestilence that stalks in darkness, nor the destruction that wastes at noonday. A thousand may fall at your side, ten thousand at your right hand, but it will not come near you. You will only look with your eyes and see the recompense of the wicked. Because you have made the Lord your dwelling place— the Most High, who is my refuge— no evil shall be allowed to befall you, no plague come near your tent. For he will command his angels concerning you to guard you in all your ways. On their hands they will bear you up, lest you strike your foot against a stone. You will tread on the lion and the adder; the young lion and the serpent you will trample underfoot. "Because he holds fast to me in love, I will deliver him; I will protect him, because he knows my name. When he calls to me, I will answer him; I will be with him in trouble; I will rescue him and honor him. With long life I will satisfy him and show him my salvation."

Psalm 91 ESV

READ all of Psalm 91.

WRITE Psalm 91:1-2 as your own prayer today.

RESPOND to what God is stirring up in you. Maybe it's been awhile since you felt close enough to hear His invitation. Repent and ask Him to forgive you for turning away from intimacy with Him. He is a faithful and loving father. He doesn't lay shame upon us. He lifts the shame off. Allow Him to do that right now.

Take a moment to recall moments that God has invited you to dwell in His presence in the middle of a trial. Write those stories down and thank God for His life-long invitation to come close to Him. Remember a time when you experienced the rest that comes from being in the shadow of the Almighty. What does that mean? It means to be so covered by His presence that you are overshadowed by it. What a beautiful picture God gives us of His presence overshadowing whatever we might be facing.

PRAY and ask God to show you this week how you can walk in this daily. Commit to memory those two verses this week. Each week, we will build on them.

PSALM 91

PSALM 91

"For he will deliver you from the snare of the fowler and from the deadly pestilence. He will cover you with his pinions, and under his wings you will find refuge; his faithfulness is a shield and buckler. You will not fear the terror of the night, nor the arrow that flies by day, nor the pestilence that stalks in darkness, nor the destruction that wastes at noonday."

Psalm 91:3-6 ESV

The imagery in this passage is a picture for us of what the protection of God looks like. The reality that we live with is, as 1 Peter 5:8-10 (ESV) tells us, "Be sober-minded; be watchful. Your adversary the devil prowls around like a roaring lion, seeking someone to devour. Resist him, firm in your faith, knowing that the same kinds of suffering are being experienced by your brotherhood throughout the world. And after you have suffered a little while, the God of all grace, who has called you to his eternal glory in Christ, will himself restore, confirm, strengthen, and establish you."

As much as we would prefer to forget, the reality is that we have an adversary. He is an opponent in this conflict we live in the tension of, here on the earth. We feel it stretching us day-by-day as we live in the victory of heaven; in the here now, but not yet. Like many of you, I feel my body, soul, and spirit caught in the tension. But the instruction of the word of God is my lifeline for navigating the treacherous landscape. When we trust in God's word, there is a safe path to travel as we navigate this territory. There is a roadmap for success available, but we must read it and trust Him to be able to live it out. We must choose Him as our guide to enjoy the safety of His pathway.

What is the pathway like? Psalm 91 gives us a play-by-play, an insight into what we might face, and how we can face it all. It's like a bright orange sign on the highway warning that there is an uneven road or bump ahead. Psalm 91 tells us there are traps set for us on the journey, not just traps but also snares. Why is that important? It's important because there are traps that we can't see on the surface but that lay ready to trip us up. But fear not. There is one who can lead you safely around them. He alone can see the traps when you cannot. Trust Him to help you through. Trust His gentle directions as you navigate the road ahead. Next on the road, The Bible talks about deadly pestilence. Exciting, right? What is deadly pestilence? It's translated for us as disease or famine that wrecks an entire community. There's no mincing words here and it's pretty obvious they aren't selling this pathway on vacations.com anytime soon. What a passage to read after the last years we have walked through as a community. Even when the enemy has us in the throws of war, we can take refuge under the shadow of the Almighty's wings. In this Psalm, the realities of the road alongside the promises of God are laid bare before us. It is the way God has chosen to include us in this mystery of salvation. We were never promised a perfect life this side of heaven, but we were given a perfect Savior to save us from an eternity of adversaries through Jesus and His blood shed for us on the cross. With this understanding of how God will give us rest even in the midst of the trials, we read on to these next verses with an understanding of how we find peace in the middle of the journey.

"We must choose Him as our guide to enjoy the safety of His pathway."

Here is our promise: He will cover you with His pinions, or feathers, and under His wings you will find refuge. His faithfulness is a shield and a buckler. Have you ever snuggled up under a comforter in the middle of a storm? You know the moment - the perfect comfort. The rain is falling, the thunder and lightning rolling and cracking through the sky, and you settle into the coziness of the blanket. The thing about getting to that place of perfect comfort is you actually have to choose to be there. That moment of crawling in to the fresh sheets and warm covers is bliss! The covering of God is this for our soul, but we have to make the choice to get under it. You might be thinking, but how? By meditating on His word (Ps. 1:2), prayer (Ps. 91:15), worship (Ps 34:1-4), journaling or writing down the promises He has spoken over you in His word and by His Holy Spirit (2 Corinthians 1:20-22). God's covering is always available to us, the question is will we choose to find shelter under it? So we know He will cover us, now let's talk about His faithfulness.

I am so thankful for His faithfulness. It is who He has always been, who He says He is, and who He will always be. His faithfulness marks our pathway as memorial stones for us to look back on and remember His goodness. They are our, "He has done it before and will do it again!" His faithfulness is our testimony and our testimony prophesies to our future, "Do it again, Lord!" The faithfulness of God is your defense. It is a defense to protect you from whatever the adversary throws at you. The thing I have learned about a shield is that it is pretty useless, unless you are behind it. You have to choose to put yourself behind the shield and buckler of His faithfulness. The way He has rescued His people since the beginning of time will again be the way He rescues you today, tomorrow, and every day after. He is a defense around you.

How? In His faithfulness. Do you want to know how He will protect you? Begin by looking back at how He has rescued and saved in the past. Look to Jesus. Do you want to get behind the shield, to be covered? Go to His word, pray, worship, and listen to Him leading and guiding you.

There might be a war raging right now, but you don't have to be afraid. You don't have to fear. Not in the night, not in the day, not the things you cannot see or the attacks that come in the wide open. You DO NOT have to be afraid. You can be covered and you can be shielded. You are invited into the safety of His refuge today.

"He who dwells in the shelter of the Most High will abide in the shadow of the Almighty. I will say to the Lord, "My refuge and my fortress, my God, in whom I trust." For he will deliver you from the snare of the fowler and from the deadly pestilence. He will cover you with his pinions, and under his wings you will find refuge; his faithfulness is a shield and buckler. You will not fear the terror of the night, nor the arrow that flies by day, nor the pestilence that stalks in darkness, nor the destruction that wastes at noonday. A thousand may fall at your side, ten thousand at your right hand, but it will not come near you. You will only look with your eyes and see the recompense of the wicked. Because you have made the Lord your dwelling place— the Most High, who is my refuge— no evil shall be allowed to befall you, no plague come near your tent. For he will command his angels concerning you to guard you in all your ways. On their hands they will bear you up, lest you strike your foot against a stone. You will tread on the lion and the adder; the young lion and the serpent you will trample underfoot. "Because he holds fast to me in love, I will deliver him; I will protect him, because he knows my name. When he calls to me, I will answer him; I will be with him in trouble; I will rescue him and honor him. With long life I will satisfy him and show him my salvation."

Psalm 91 ESV

READ all of Psalm 91.

WRITE Psalm 91:3-6 as your own prayer today.

RESPOND and take a moment to recall moments that God delivered you in the middle of a storm, or a time when you felt yourself safe under His covering. Write the stories in your own life when the war was raging and the faithfulness of God rescued you. Maybe you're in the middle of a storm now. Begin to remind yourself how God has been faithful and let it become a shield and buckler for this very moment. You can trust Him. He has been faithful before and He will be again.

What is God stirring up in you. Is fear something you struggle with? Ask God to help you and show you how you can trust Him. Tell fear it has to leave because you have a faithful God. Remind your soul today who your God is and begin to thank Him for who He is.

PRAY and ask God to show you this week how you can walk in this daily. Commit to memory those verses this week. We will continue building on them every week.

PSALM 91

PSALM 91

THREE

"A thousand may fall at your side, ten thousand at your right hand, but it will not come near you. You will only look with your eyes and see the recompense of the wicked. Because you have made the Lord your dwelling place— the Most High, who is my refuge— no evil shall be allowed to befall you, no plague come near your tent. For he will command his angels concerning you to guard you in all your ways. On their hands they will bear you up, lest you strike your foot against a stone. You will tread on the lion and the adder; the young lion and the serpent you will trample underfoot."

Psalm 91:7-13 ESV

I love Florida. I am a Florida girl through and through, but there is one season that tests my love for this beautiful place every year - mosquito season. If you know, you know. I am one of those people that mosquitos love. My momma used to tell me it was because I was so sweet and I definitely believed her. Since those days, I've read articles and research about the reasons those obnoxious little insects like or don't like one person to the next, and I've learned there are lots of reasons those little pests like me more. Truth be told, I don't mind pretending it really is just because I'm sweet!

You might be asking yourself the question, "Why are we starting with mosquitos?" I have this visual in my mind of being outside on the back porch in the heat of late summer with my friend and whilst I am being annihilated by mosquito bites with everyone else, one cheeky guest perks up and says, "I don't know what you're talking about. They aren't biting me!"

It's a silly parallel but you can see it, right? Wouldn't it be nice to be the one that the sting never touched? What a safe and secure place of refuge that would be. Oh, the feeling of being protected and covered in the middle of attack. This is what it's like to be in the shelter and dwelling of God most High. When we dwell with Him, when we are under His covering and trusting in His faithfulness - things might seem like they are falling apart all around us, but you and I are held together. Not in our own strength, but in His. God of the angel armies will command His angels concerning us to guard us and keep us from harm. When there are poisonous attacks against us, we can trust that we are protected. While the world might try and convince us that we should be overwhelmed, we face the challenge with the Prince of Peace, JESUS, living in our hearts. Even when we experience the effects of sin on the earth, of a broken world, we get to stand up and SHOUT the victory of Jesus - of heaven and home that await us even beyond the grave (Rev. 21:4). We have an eternal hope. We are victorious in Christ. There is nothing that can separate us from His love. Even in the midst of a battle, we stand as overcoming by the blood of the Lamb and the word of our testimony (Rev. 12:11).

The last part of these verses we are reading today finish with our steps. Did you know your steps are established by the Lord?

"The steps of a man are established by the Lord, when he delights in his way; though he fall, he shall not be cast headlong, for the Lord upholds his hand." (Psalm 37:23-24)

When we delight in His way, we find ourselves enjoying the trust that comes with believing in our hearts that He has set the path before us. We may encounter lion and serpent, but He will protect us. No fang nor poison will break through to harm because He has already established the path. We don't have to stop walking forward on the path because a lion or serpent has come into it trying to convince us the way is blocked or unsafe. We keep walking, knowing that those barricades will become merely a mat under our feet. In other words, the enemy doesn't get to redirect our path. Fear doesn't get to take us captive when we trust in God (Psalm 56:3, Joshua 1:9, Psalm 118:6, Proverbs 29:25). He might try the tactic of fear, but we can remember this truth - we will tread on fear like the defeated enemy it is.

"The Lord is my light and my salvation; whom shall I fear? The Lord is the stronghold of my life; of whom shall I be afraid? When evildoers assail me to eat up my flesh, my adversaries and foes, it is they who stumble and fall. Though an army encamp against me, my heart shall not fear; though war arise against me, yet I will be confident."
Psalm 27:1-3 ESV

"He who dwells in the shelter of the Most High will abide in the shadow of the Almighty. I will say to the Lord, "My refuge and my fortress, my God, in whom I trust." For he will deliver you from the snare of the fowler and from the deadly pestilence. He will cover you with his pinions, and under his wings you will find refuge; his faithfulness is a shield and buckler. You will not fear the terror of the night, nor the arrow that flies by day, nor the pestilence that stalks in darkness, nor the destruction that wastes at noonday. A thousand may fall at your side, ten thousand at your right hand, but it will not come near you. You will only look with your eyes and see the recompense of the wicked. Because you have made the Lord your dwelling place— the Most High, who is my refuge— no evil shall be allowed to befall you, no plague come near your tent. For he will command his angels concerning you to guard you in all your ways. On their hands they will bear you up, lest you strike your foot against a stone. You will tread on the lion and the adder; the young lion and the serpent you will trample underfoot. "Because he holds fast to me in love, I will deliver him; I will protect him, because he knows my name. When he calls to me, I will answer him; I will be with him in trouble; I will rescue him and honor him. With long life I will satisfy him and show him my salvation."

Psalm 91 ESV

READ all of Psalm 91.

WRITE Psalm 91:7-13 as your own prayer today.

RESPOND and take a moment to recall moments that you saw the battle raging around you and realized you were pulled in close, under the shadow of the wings of God Almighty. Was there a moment when you felt like it was impossible that even in the middle of a storm, you were somehow okay? Was there a moment you felt like you were shouting victory as you tread on the enemy on the pathway God had set before you?

Write down those stories and moments. Maybe you are in one right now. Maybe you need to testify to your own soul that God will come through today as He has in the past. If you can't think of your own story right now, open the word of God and begin to read stories of His faithfulness to His chosen people in the Old Testament or the stories throughout the New Testament, the Acts of the Apostles or the miraculous growth of churches in the epistles. Let the victory we have in Jesus echo in your heart and from your mouth today.

PRAY and ask God to show you how to live today as one protected from the battle. Pray that He would give you boldness to tread on the lion and serpent as you confidently walk the path He's laid out before you.

PSALM 91

PSALM 91

FOUR

"Because he holds fast to me in love, I will deliver him; I will protect him, because he knows my name. When he calls to me, I will answer him; I will be with him in trouble; I will rescue him and honor him. With long life I will satisfy him and show him my salvation."

Psalm 91:14-16 ESV

Have you ever been stuck in a tree? As a child, I used to climb trees all the time and as I was learning to go higher and higher, there were many times I would find myself climbing beyond my skill level and shouting from the higher limbs, "I can't get down!" Looking hopefully at the ground below, I would scan the yard and with a slightly panicked cry, keep calling out "I can't get down" until my dad, mom or anyone who looked able to help me out of the tree came to my rescue. The scariest part of the whole ordeal wasn't even getting stuck. It was the moment you had to let go of the tree and trust the person helping you down to carry your weight to the ground. It seemed so far to trust, such a drop to just let go, and be caught. I held on for dear life as I let go of the tree and relied completely on my rescuers arms.

We have a rescuer. We have a Savior whose arms stretched wide for us - to save us from a place we could never be freed from on our own. I wonder if sometimes, from our place of slight panic, we look at the deliverer and are just too afraid to truly let go and trust His arms to catch us. I wonder if sometimes we sit on the limbs of our own merit and call out wondering if He really will show up for us, or if we have gone too far this time for His arms to reach.

Did you know that He has been coming to our rescue long before we ever knew we needed it? When God sent His only Son, Jesus, to die on the cross for our sins, to give us the opportunity to believe in Him, He did that long before you and I took our first breath. We hadn't even come into the world, and yet He came into the world so that we might have life. He knew we would be people of adventure and wonder. He knew we would want to stretch to the boundary lines of all that was before us. He knew we wouldn't be perfect, and that we would need grace over and over. In all of this,

He planned on hearing our cry for help and responding. Not just that, but He went beyond response to relationship. He bestows honor on us and He satisfies us by giving our lives the kind of longevity that is not length of days, but fullness of joy in them by His Spirit and His power.

"We have a Savior whose arms stretched wide for us - to save us from a place we could never be freed from on our own."

"He who dwells in the shelter of the Most High will abide in the shadow of the Almighty. I will say to the Lord, "My refuge and my fortress, my God, in whom I trust." For he will deliver you from the snare of the fowler and from the deadly pestilence. He will cover you with his pinions, and under his wings you will find refuge; his faithfulness is a shield and buckler. You will not fear the terror of the night, nor the arrow that flies by day, nor the pestilence that stalks in darkness, nor the destruction that wastes at noonday. A thousand may fall at your side, ten thousand at your right hand, but it will not come near you. You will only look with your eyes and see the recompense of the wicked. Because you have made the Lord your dwelling place— the Most High, who is my refuge— no evil shall be allowed to befall you, no plague come near your tent. For he will command his angels concerning you to guard you in all your ways. On their hands they will bear you up, lest you strike your foot against a stone. You will tread on the lion and the adder; the young lion and the serpent you will trample underfoot. "Because he holds fast to me in love, I will deliver him; I will protect him, because he knows my name. When he calls to me, I will answer him; I will be with him in trouble; I will rescue him and honor him. With long life I will satisfy him and show him my salvation."

Psalm 91 ESV

READ all of Psalm 91.

WRITE Psalm 91:24-16 as your own prayer today.

RESPOND and take a moment to recall a time when you cried out to God to rescue you. How did He show up? Did you get an answer right away? If not, what did He teach you in the waiting? His response to your cry today is not flippant or half-hearted. He knew you would cry out long before you took your first breath and He knew how He would respond. He is not last minute. He is not rushing to make it in time. He is everywhere always and He is ready to be your rescuer. He delights in coming as your help in time of trouble (Psalm 46:1).

Write down those stories and moments. Has it been hard for you to trust that He will respond when you call? Tell Him that. Ask Him to help you trust Him. Remind yourself right now of how He has been faithful in the past when you have cried out to Him for help. Are you in a season of already celebrating how He has come to your rescue? Thank Him. Rejoice in His rescue. Tell Him you are thankful. Exalt His name. No matter what place you find yourself in today - He has not changed. He remains the rescuer and the helper of His people.

PRAY Today, we lift our praise to our God who is faithful to respond. Extol His name, glorify the Lord for who He is and what He has done, is doing, and will do. He will not fail you. He will honor you as He rescues you and delivers you with life and salvation. It is His word that bears this promise for us today.

PSALM
23

The Lord is my shepherd; I shall not want. He makes me lie down in green pastures. He leads me beside still waters. He restores my soul. He leads me in paths of righteousness for his name's sake. Even though I walk through the valley of the shadow of death, I will fear no evil, for you are with me; your orod and your staff, they comfort me. You prepare a table before me in the presence of my enemies; you anoint my head with oil; my cup overflows. Surely goodness and mercy shall follow me all the days of my life, and I shall dwell in the house of the LORD forever.

Psalm 23 ESV

ONE

"The Lord is my shepherd; I shall not want. He makes me lie down in green pastures. He leads me beside still waters. He restores my soul. He leads me in paths of righteousness for his name's sake."

Psalm 23:1-3 ESV

This is probably one of the most familiar Psalms in our Bible. Many of us have heard it our whole lives. It is, perhaps, most well-known for being a Psalm of comfort in time of loss. I have wept as I've heard it read over too many lost friends and family members through the years. I would dare to say we all have a story we can attach to this Psalm and most of us could quote at least a line or two from memory. These words penned from heavens vault of truth and mercy, the true and inspired word of God, are a balm on the wounds of the hurting. They are mercy to the hearts of the grieving. They are a confession of truth in time of trouble. We read in Psalm 23 who our God is and understand that because God is, therefore I am. He is my Shepherd, therefore I lack nothing. It is because of who He is that we can confidently be who we are called to be. It resonates with our statement that we began this journey with - if not for You. A reminder to our hearts that it is because of who He is that we are who we are.

He is our Shepherd.

A good shepherd cares for their sheep. Not only does a shepherd love their sheep but our good Shepherd knows each of His sheep by name. A good Shepherd cares for and protects each sheep. Let that sink in. Selah (pause and think about it). He knows your name. He is the King of Kings and Lord of Lords. He is the ruler over all and the one who was and is and is to come, and yet He knows your name.

Jesus, our Good Shepherd, tells a parable in Luke 15 that describes the care of a shepherd.

""What man of you, having a hundred sheep, if he has lost one of them, does not leave the ninety-nine in the open country, and go after the one that is lost, until he finds it? And when he has found it, he lays it on his shoulders, rejoicing. And when he comes home, he calls together his friends and his neighbors, saying to them, 'Rejoice with me, for I have found my sheep that was lost.' Just so, I tell you, there will be more joy in heaven over one sinner who repents than over ninety-nine righteous persons who need no repentance." (Luke 15:4-7 ESV)

We have a good Shepherd, He knows us by name and He cares for us.

We have a Shepherd and it is because of this Shepherd we begin this study of Psalm 23 by writing this phrase, "I shall not want." I know this Good Shepherd has everything that I need - I will never be lacking any good thing (Philippians 4:13).

"The Lord is my shepherd; I shall not want. He makes me lie down in green pastures. He leads me beside still waters. He restores my soul. He leads me in paths of righteousness for his name's sake." Psalm 23:1-3 ESV

If you look at the hills of Israel and study where the shepherds would lead and graze their sheep, you find something very different than you probably grew up imagining. We read, "He makes me lie down in green pastures," and think of lush green fields, right? I certainly always have, but did you know our western version of green pastures is very different than the version the Bible is talking about here, and what David would likely have been referring to? It would have been rare to find a shepherd who was frequently able to lead their sheep to the green meadows where the sheep would eat until they were full and then lie down to rest, satisfied. David would more likely have had to lead his sheep as a shepherd, roaming hills and valleys, in more remote and rugged regions. Canaan was a good land, a place of blessing for God's people, but the best lands - the areas with the most rainfall were reserved for agriculture. If you go to Israel today and find the shepherds grazing their sheep, you won't find the rolling green hills you have probably always pictured in your mind. You'll find dust and rock filled dirt and a land that receives only a total of around 23 inches of rain per year. On a closer inspection of these hills, you will find small tufts of grass sparsely coating the steep grades. These morsels of nourishment are born from the humidity that comes across the Mediterranean and coats the hillside overnight. As the condensation erupts from the rock, the tufts of grass are born near it, causing there to form small patches of green for each day.

"He is with us every step of the journey."

In the hillsides of Israel, you will find the sheep are being led by a shepherd to the grass that will sustain them for today. Even more accurately, one bite at a time. I think I've always imagined getting escorted like a celebrity to my green pastures. I lay down in the cool grass and enjoy the benefits of the land, but if I'm honest after getting there the thought of the shepherd sort of leaves my mind. In this biblical scenario, the shepherd never leaves the sheep. The reality is the sheep need help to get up and down the rocky mountain. The sheep need help knowing where the next patch of grass is and how to navigate the steep mountainside by often circling around and around to come back down to safety. The sheep are never in a place where they don't need to rely on the shepherd to show them what's next. In parallel to our own lives, I believe there are times when we can imagine ourselves giving God some sort of break from leading us as He leaves us in our lush fields to fend for ourselves, when in reality that's not what a shepherd does with His sheep. He is with us every step of the journey.

This is one of our greatest challenges. I don't know about you, but I tend to get to a place of comfort and begin to rely on myself and because I have a loving Father in heaven, He begins to teach me yet again that there isn't a day or season that I find myself without need of Him. We need our Shepherd every day leading and guiding us. We need our Shepherd to show us where we will be sustained. Does this remind you at all of manna in the desert? He gives us what we need for today, so we remember to stay close and trust Him to provide what we need for tomorrow. I have too often, throughout my life, found myself having forgotten where the bread of life comes from.

"Then Jesus declared, "I am the bread of life. Whoever comes to me will never go hungry, and whoever believes in me will never be thirsty." John 6:35 NIV

I don't ever want to get to a place where I find myself forgetting my desperate need for my Shepherd.

"The Lord is my shepherd; I shall not want. He makes me lie down in green pastures. He leads me beside still waters. He restores my soul. He leads me in paths of righteousness for his name's sake. Even though I walk through the valley of the shadow of death, I will fear no evil, for you are with me; your rod and your staff, they comfort me. You prepare a table before me in the presence of my enemies; you anoint my head with oil; my cup overflows. Surely goodness and mercy shall follow me all the days of my life, and I shall dwell in the house of the Lord forever."

Psalm 23 ESV

READ all of Psalm 23.

WRITE this down in your own words: The Lord is my Shepherd.

RESPOND Where has God has been leading you?
Is there a place in your life where you have been trying to sustain yourself? Confess it to God and ask for forgiveness. Ask Him to help you to rely on Him for what you need.
Where you are challenged today to trust Him more?

PRAY and ask God to help you see Him as the Shepherd. Praise Him for the way He has always provided what you need. Pray that He will help you to trust Him to lead you safely where you are called to be.

PSALM 23

PSALM 23

"The Lord is my shepherd; I shall not want. He makes me lie down in green pastures. He leads me beside still waters. He restores my soul. He leads me in paths of righteousness for his name's sake."

Psalm 23:1-3 ESV

He leads me beside still waters.

"The Lord is my shepherd; I shall not want. He makes me lie down in green pastures. He leads me beside still waters. He restores my soul. He leads me in paths of righteousness for his name's sake."
Psalm 23:1-3 ESV

Have you ever felt your body craving water? Think about it. You know that feeling, right? Maybe after a work out, or mid-day when you've just neglected to give your body what it needs. There is a parched and needy feeling that quickly turns to desperation if your need for water isn't quenched. Water is essential to our lives and bodies. You cannot survive without water. Similarly, our spiritual lives thirst for water and the Bible is very clear on where it comes from.

"Jesus said to her, "Everyone who drinks of this water will be thirsty again, but whoever drinks of the water that I will give him will never be thirsty again. The water that I will give him will become in him a spring of water welling up to eternal life.""
John 4:13-14 ESV

There is a source of water that never runs out for us and He is alive in us today. This Psalm reminds us how He leads us to still waters. The Hebrew word for still waters is "Mai Menochot." It literally means restful waters. A place to rest in knowing that He is enough. We don't need to be ready for a chaotic torrent of water to give us what we need, or even the putrid waters from a stagnant lake. He leads us to a gently flowing place of rest and refreshment. He knows the perfect place on the path to take us to find rest.
In Matthew 11:28 (NIV), Jesus tells us: ""Come to me, all you who are weary and burdened, and I will give you rest."

He leads us where we can find what we desperately need to be fully alive. He doesn't just guide us to water that will run out, but He became for us a spring of living water bubbling up from within us. He fills us with His presence when we invite Him to live inside our hearts and He restores us from the inside out.

If you look at the hillsides of Israel that we learned about in part one, you will notice a weaving path along the mountains. It is a circular pathway leading downwards or upwards and the paths cross in an almost maze-like fashion. It looks similar to a maze you might give a child to do. The reality is we need a Shepherd to lead us on paths of righteousness. The paths we face in life can often feel like a maze. Which one do I take? They all seem so similar and I'm going down when I thought this one would take me upwards. The good Shepherd knows the paths ahead. We can trust the Shepherd to lead us up and down the mountain at the right time. We love the Shepherd and we want to follow wherever He is leading us for His names sake.

What paths of righteousness is the Shepherd asking you to walk today? I have found over the years that I will sense the calling of the Shepherd, righteous and holy, walking the road with me. As He calls me to come with Him on the journey, I'm faced with every day choices to simply say, "Yes, Lord." There are certainly moments of great importance - the big decisions of life along the journey that require our "yes" to Him, but the "yes" moments we face in the small areas of life are the steps that get us to the paths of Psalm 23. Our lives, lived as acts of surrender and worship, are the substance of the paths (Romans 12:1-2). The big moments are memorial stones marking the paths of righteousness, but the path itself is often made up of the uncelebrated, every day, surrender moments to the Shepherd.

“The Lord is my shepherd; I shall not want. He makes me lie down in green pastures. He leads me beside still waters. He restores my soul. He leads me in paths of righteousness for his name’s sake. Even though I walk through the valley of the shadow of death, I will fear no evil, for you are with me; your rod and your staff, they comfort me. You prepare a table before me in the presence of my enemies; you anoint my head with oil; my cup overflows. Surely goodness and mercy shall follow me all the days of my life, and I shall dwell in the house of the Lord forever.”

Psalm 23 ESV

READ all of Psalm 23.

WRITE this down in your own words: Wherever you lead, I'll go.

RESPOND Where has God been stirring your heart to surrender fully and say 'yes' to Him? Where are you challenged today to trust Him more?

PRAY and remind your soul of God's faithfulness to give you all you need. Remember a time when you hungered and thirsted for Him (Psalm 63:1). Remind yourself of His faithfulness. Thank God for a path that includes His presence as our Shepherd.

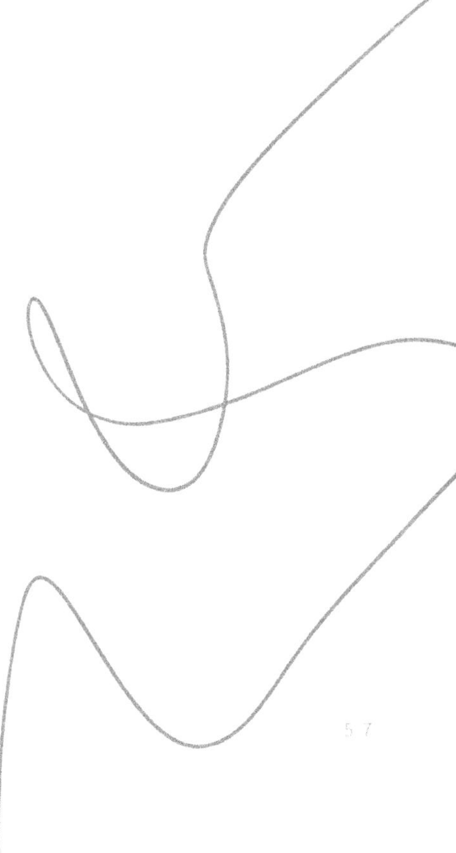

PSALM 23

PSALM 23

THREE

"Even though I walk through the valley of the shadow of death, I will fear no evil, for you are with me; your rod and your staff, they comfort me."

Psalm 23:4 ESV

Even though, Lord. Even when, Lord. Even if, Lord. It is an arresting thought. To choose, ahead of time, the kind of submission that confesses these words. We know that as we navigate this life, it is not that we might have troubles, but that we will have troubles (John 16:33). I don't know about you, but what better choice than to resolve in our hearts that before the heartache comes we will trust in God. To resolve that EVEN THOUGH I walk through the valley of the shadow of death; I will trust you to be there with me, Lord.

No shadow exists without light. Imagine a valley between two mountains, the sun breaking just at eyes reach. We can often be in the valley and because we cannot feel the warmth of the sun on our skin, we begin to believe that it exists only as a reminder of what we cannot have. As if the sun were taunting us from just over the mountain: the shadowed valley, cold and bare, our captor. This is the kind of thinking that tells us we should take up residence in the valley. This is the kind of thinking that tells us that the warmth of the sun on our skin will always be just out of reach. This is the kind of thinking that convinces us that the sackcloth and ashes of grief will forever be our portion. They are not. Let your heart receive that today. Our God is a God of hope. He makes beauty from ashes, removes our sackcloth of mourning, and trades it for joy.

"The Spirit of the Sovereign Lord is on me, because the Lord has anointed me to proclaim good news to the poor. He has sent me to bind up the brokenhearted, to proclaim freedom for the captives and release from darkness for the prisoners, to proclaim the year of the Lord s favor and the day of vengeance of our God, to comfort all who mourn, and provide for those who grieve in Zion– to bestow on them a crown of beauty instead of ashes, the oil of joy instead

of mourning, and a garment of praise instead of a spirit of despair. They will be called oaks of righteousness, a planting of the Lord for the display of his splendor. They will rebuild the ancient ruins and restore the places long devastated; they will renew the ruined cities that have been devastated for generations."
Isaiah 61:1-4 NIV

Psalm 23 is a reminder that there are seasons in life. Here, in Florida, it feels like eternal summer most of the time. Aside

"He makes beauty from ashes, removes our sackcloth of mourning, and trades it for joy."

from the brief reprieve in the short couple of months where the temperature gage falls just below 70, we are blessed to feel the warmth of the sun most days. As a native Floridian, I know that once the winter chill comes and I'm aching for the warmth of the sun again I just have to press on and push through because it wont be long. I have lived in NYC and the pressing on took a bit longer. Instead of a couple of months of the chill hitting my face, it was an extended season of bitter cold. I have friends in Canada that experience the cold for longer seasons than I ever have. Why include seasons as we walk through Psalm 23? Because some valleys take longer to navigate than others. Some winters last longer than others. There are times when you are aching for the sun to warm your face again and it feels like it will never happen. Hold on to hope. The season will change and you will walk from the shadowed valley into the warmth of the sun again.

"Let us hold unswervingly to the hope we profess, for he who promised is faithful. And let us consider how we may spur one another on toward love and good deeds, not giving up meeting together, as some are in the habit of doing, but encouraging one another–and all the more as you see the Day approaching."
Hebrews 10:23-25 NIV

Jesus is the hope of the earth. Jesus is the light of the world. Under the old covenant the people of God hoped in God, heard from Him through a select few, and lived on memories of faithfulness, sacrifices, and hope for the future. They didn't have access as we do to God their Father. Only a few heard from Him, only a few experienced closeness to His presence. We live under a new covenant and we have the living God walking with us. We hope as hope walks beside us, speaking into our hearts, showing us the way forward in the valley. We don't have to make it our home or take up residence there (Hebrews 6:19, Ephesians 2:11-22 NIV). When you walk through the valley, He is with you. He even makes crooked paths straight (Proverbs 3:6). He is close to the broken-hearted (Psalm 34:18). He's not only with you in the valley, but He doesn't plan on keeping you there. He is leading you out to the warmth of the sun again. Anchor your soul to hope, to Jesus, and let Him lead you through.

"The Lord is my shepherd; I shall not want. He makes me lie down in green pastures. He leads me beside still waters. He restores my soul. He leads me in paths of righteousness for his name's sake. Even though I walk through the valley of the shadow of death, I will fear no evil, for you are with me; your rod and your staff, they comfort me. You prepare a table before me in the presence of my enemies; you anoint my head with oil; my cup overflows. Surely goodness and mercy shall follow me all the days of my life, and I shall dwell in the house of the Lord forever."

Psalm 23 ESV

READ all of Psalm 23.

WRITE this down in your own words: Even if, even when, even though I walk through the valley, you are with me.

RESPOND What valley have you come through in your life that you can remember God's closeness and faithfulness in? Write down a time you have navigated a valley without looking to Him and the difference that you experience as you navigate a valley clinging to Him.

PRAY God, when life is not what I expected or painful and bitter - you are not waiting at the end of my pain, you are with me in it. Thank you that you don't leave me alone in the valley. Thank you that the valley is not my home. Thank you, God, that today you lead me onwards and are in the process of calling me homewards in Christ Jesus. (Philippians 3:14 NIV, 2 Timothy 1:9 NIV)

PSALM 23

FOUR

"Even though I walk through the valley of the shadow of death, I will fear no evil, for you are with me;
your rod and your staff, they
comfort me."

Psalm 23:4 ESV

There is a reason that we do not have to be afraid in the valley and the description for us to wrap our minds around is found here, in the presence of the Lord with us and in the rod and the staff He wields. The Lord with me is a thought that brings thankfulness and comfort. What a thought - that the God of all creation would be with us. As we read on, I must confess that when I'm thinking about comfort, the first description of a comforting object isn't a rod and a staff. As a matter of fact, it is quite the opposite of what I would consider comfortable. But it it is what David describes as a comfort to himself. I don't need to fear FOR YOU ARE WITH ME. Your rod and your staff, they comfort me.

A shepherd in this time would have carried both a rod and staff as they went about their work. The rod and staff were essential to them. I used to imagine the rod and staff as a tool to cause the sheep to submit, the staff a hook as in the old comedy films sweeping around the neck of an unsuspecting thespian and dragging them in humiliation off the stage. Once again, in study I have found my western view of these objects led me to relate my experience of those tools to a scenario in which my experiences created an incorrect view of what was actually happening in this text. When we put ourselves in the shoes of a shepherd, we find that the tools had a different purpose. The rod was a sturdy stick. It's purpose to fight off wild animals looking to attack defenseless sheep. The rod helped the shepherd to keep track of the sheep, to make sure they were all accounted for. We can see in the scripture where the rod was likely used to rescue the sheep.

"But David said to Saul, "Your servant used to keep sheep for his father. And when there came a lion, or a bear, and took a lamb from the flock, I went after him and struck him and delivered it out of his mouth. And if he arose against me, I caught him by his beard and

struck him and killed him."
1 Samuel 17:34-35 ESV
The rod is comforting because it represents the defense and care of the sheep. In the wrong hands, it could become a source of pain for the sheep. But our Good Shepherd has the rod that defends us. He has and is thwarting dangers that come in the night, in the day, and in the valley. He is wielding it as one who watches over and cares for His sheep. Think about that. He is your defender. He is your protector. He is defending YOU. When He tells us not to worry about tomorrow (Matthew 6:34 ESV) and worry tries to overtake us, we can imagine our Good Shepherd - rod in hand - defending us through the watches of the night and into the dawn breaking over the horizon.

The shepherds staff, in rhythm with the rod, is essential to the shepherd. It serves as a guide, a slender stick with a hook directing the sheep to what they need. The thing about sheep (and if I'm honest, I see myself too easily in this thought) is that they wander. They are prone to wander. The old hymn resounds in my mind thinking of my tendency to wander and be distracted, often making a mess of my life.

"Oh, to grace how great a debtor
daily I'm constrained to be!
Let thy goodness, like a fetter,
bind my wandering heart to thee:
prone to wander, Lord, I feel it,
prone to leave the God I love;
here's my heart, O take and seal it;
seal it for thy courts above."

AUTHOR: ROBERT ROBINSON, PUBLIC DOMAIN

The staff was a tool to keep the sheep close to the shepherd. While I imagine the looping of the staffs hook around the neck of the sheep a humiliation for the sheep; I miss the beauty of the sheep being in a precarious or deadly situation and being rescued by the hook. Isn't it all too painfully true that we find ourselves faced with the rescue from our Good Shepherd and in our pride we won't let Him use the tools He needs to save us from ourselves? Too often, pride keeps us from embracing the work of our Savior. It's been true in my own life. I have found myself forgetting the leading of the Shepherd in seasons past simply because pride takes first place and leaves me out on a limb too arrogant to let the Shepherd wrap His staff around my neck and bring me to safety. The irony is that my wandering is what found me in need of rescue in the first place.

The shepherds staff couldn't be used on any other animal. It was made for the sheep. The sheep need the experience and eyes of the shepherd watching over them ready to wield the staff. You and I need to embrace the Good Shepherd and His correction and salvation. I believe that sometimes we think we are the Shepherd instead of the sheep, and find ourselves trying to wield a tool we were never meant to hold.

The rod and the staff are a well-known symbol of the shepherd. This is our comfort. When we experience protection and guidance, we can know the Shepherd is with us, He is around us, and He is for us.

"The Lord is my shepherd; I shall not want. He makes me lie down in green pastures. He leads me beside still waters. He restores my soul. He leads me in paths of righteousness for his name's sake. Even though I walk through the valley of the shadow of death, I will fear no evil, for you are with me; your rod and your staff, they comfort me. You prepare a table before me in the presence of my enemies; you anoint my head with oil; my cup overflows. Surely goodness and mercy shall follow me all the days of my life, and I shall dwell in the house of the Lord forever."

Psalm 23 ESV

READ all of Psalm 23.

WRITE this down in your own words: "...for you are with me; your rod and your staff, they comfort me."

RESPOND Think about a time you felt the protection of the Shepherd. How did the 'rod' of His protection keep you safe? Can you think of a time you didn't realize that the wait you were in or the no you got from God was a rod of protection for you in the valley? What about the staff - how has He reached to pull you from a dangerous or precarious place? Write these things down and thank God that we can be comforted by His rod and staff.

PRAY Thank you, Jesus, for protection. When I cannot see all the details but know You are with me, I will trust that you are both a defense and a rescue. Help me to trust you to do both of those things. Help my unbelief. Jesus, remove the pride that is a barrier from receiving your rescue.

PSALM 23

FIVE

"You prepare a table before me in the presence of my enemies; you anoint my head with oil; my cup overflows. Surely goodness and mercy shall follow me all the days of my life, and I shall dwell in the house of the Lord forever."

Psalm 23:5-6 ESV

It is a wild thought to imagine the Lord setting the table. What a beautiful picture of the victory of our Lord. While in the middle of battle, in the presence of enemies wanting to attack us, we are invited to sit at the table of the Lord. To receive what He has prepared for us.

If there is one thing I'm not great at, it's pausing in the middle of battle. Whether it is the battle of the piles of laundry that overtake my home every week, the cleaning, the errands, the to-do lists, the work or the taxi service I provide to my children - often the first thing to go from my priority list in my battle of busy is the time to receive from the Lord what He has prepared for me. The truth is, all of my love for Him, my heart to worship, praise and desire to serve Him - came from HIM. I didn't muster it up on my own and I will never have the strength to continue a life of love for Him if I have not received love from Him first. "For God SO LOVED the world (John 3:16 ESV)." It came from Him first. The lesson for us here is that we must be ready in seasons of rest, valley, or enemy attack to receive from God what He wants to fill us with for

"He has already won and therefore our fight is from victory, not for victory."

whatever lies ahead. Only the Shepherd knows what we will need to for the days to come.

As we sit at the table of the Lord, which for us as New Testament believers is the table of communion, we remember that it is the blood of Jesus and His broken body, His death and resurrection, that are the only reason wc can find refreshments in seasons of battle. He has already won and therefore our fight is from victory, not for victory. It is in the emergence from the valley that we find ourselves at this table ready for what's next. Even when we are still surrounded by enemies, we can begin to live as victors, taking our rest even in the enemies presence. A sign and symbol to the defeated that we have abundant provision in the battle.

As we sit at the table and remember Jesus, Psalm 23 tells us that two things happen. He anoints our head with oil and our cup overflows. Anointing with oil represents blessing and in this passage, blessing for our entire life. So much blessing, in fact, that our cup is overflowing. This anointing isn't just a meeting of task or need but of abundance and delight. I imagine this anointing like that hair washing station at my salon. Stay with me, here. You lean back, ready to relax, and your hair is drenched with perfectly warm water. You hear the shampoo bottle pumping out the luxurious shampoo and heavenly scent you know and love. There's not just a couple of pumps like the rations you enjoy in your personal shower, there is abundance. Your hair is hardly ever as scrubbed and clean as in that salon moment. The shampoo and conditioner flow like rivers. No pump is too much. Can you see the parallel?

"See what great love the Father has lavished on us, that we should be called children of God! And that is what we are! The reason the world does not know us is that it did not know him." (1 John 3:1 NIV)

When your enemies see you at the table, you are so coated and overflowing with blessing that there is an extravagance to the way God has provided for you that is evident to all. What is the extravagance? His Holy Spirit working in and through you, His mercy and grace covering you, and His victory overshadowing you.

"He has become our home."

It is because of this unfathomable truth that we can declare, like David, "Surely goodness and mercy shall follow me all the days of my life, and I shall dwell in the house of the Lord forever." No matter what has made up the valleys of my path: His mercy and goodness were with me all along, the Good Shepherd guiding me all the way. They are like the tracks left by a vehicle through the soft sand showing that it was there. When we turn to survey the valley we have come out of in victory, we see the marks of the Shepherd at every turn and He has become our home. Savior like a Shepherd leading us in every place we have been and will be.

PSALM 23

"The Lord is my shepherd; I shall not want. He makes me lie down in green pastures. He leads me beside still waters. He restores my soul. He leads me in paths of righteousness for his name's sake. Even though I walk through the valley of the shadow of death, I will fear no evil, for you are with me; your rod and your staff, they comfort me. You prepare a table before me in the presence of my enemies; you anoint my head with oil; my cup overflows. Surely goodness and mercy shall follow me all the days of my life, and I shall dwell in the house of the Lord forever."

Psalm 23 ESV

READ all of Psalm 23.

WRITE this down in your own words: "You prepare a table before me in the presence of my enemies; you anoint my head with oil; my cup overflows. Surely goodness and mercy shall follow me all the days of my life, and I shall dwell in the house of the Lord forever."

RESPOND and thank God for the table He has set before you in this very season. Thank Him for the cross and the resurrection. Thank Him for victory in His name. Think of how He has provided even in the darkest seasons and in the presence of enemies. Write these things down. How has your life overflowed with His presence? When you look back at the seasons you have walked through, what tracks do you see of His nearness, goodness and mercy throughout the years? Take a moment to tell Him you love Him and want to dwell in His house forever.

PRAY and write out your own prayer today. How has Psalm 23 come alive in your heart and helped you to know the Lord as your Good Shepherd? Praise, repent, ask and yield as you talk to your heavenly Father.

PSALM 23

PSALM 23

PSALM
20

"May the Lord answer you in the day of trouble! May the name of the God of Jacob protect you! May he send you help from the sanctuary and give you support from Zion! May he remember all your offerings and regard with favor your burnt sacrifices! Selah. May he grant you your heart's desire and fulfill all your plans! May we shout for joy over your salvation, and in the name of our God set up our banners! May the Lord fulfill all your petitions! Now I know that the Lord saves his anointed; he will answer him from his holy heaven with the saving might of his right hand. Some trust in chariots and some in horses, but we trust in the name of the Lord our God. They collapse and fall, but we rise and stand upright. O Lord, save the king! May he answer us when we call."

Psalm 20 ESV

ONE

"May the Lord answer you in the day of trouble! May the name of the God of Jacob protect you! May he send you help from the sanctuary and give you support from Zion! May he remember all your offerings and regard with favor your burnt sacrifices! Selah."

Psalm 20:1-3 ESV

What a title to banner a Psalm. "Trust in the Name of the Lord Our God." What a banner to place over our own lives. As we begin this Psalm with a prayer, let's stop to pray now"

"God, help me to trust in Your name. Not in my own name, standing, strength or ability but in Your name."

David, who pens this Psalm, experienced days of trouble throughout his entire life. He is described as a man after God's own heart, far from perfect, but pursuing his God. He navigated days of trouble from his days in the fields fighting off bears and lions to protect his sheep. He faced trouble head on in his battle with Goliath and on to the end of his life pursued by Saul, all while trusting in God to help him, save Him, have mercy on him and lead the people of Israel. He faced dark days of trouble after falling into sin as a king and battling to lead God's people again. He was well acquainted with trouble. This wasn't just a thought for him, but a testimony and prophecy over the people of God. "May the Lord answer you in the day of trouble!"

We used to sail and spent a season enamored with it. We would watch shows about it, sail our own boat, and even had our kids in sailing lessons. Many of the shows we watched were about couples or families living aboard boats and sailing the world. What a thought! They would cast off the lines and leave the shore, relying on their research of wind, waves, and storms. Then, by the power of the wind in their sails they would make their way to the next destination. Their boats had been prepared. There were provisions for every meal and extras in case of emergency. They assigned night watches so that someone would always be on the look out in the night for ships and other hazards that could harm the boat. There were life lines and life jackets along with a small rescue device called an EPIRB. Everything on the boat aside from the EPIRB was preparation for what they would need aboard and could do for themselves to be safe. However, the EPIRB was the one device that was meant to be a connector when they couldn't help themselves anymore. It was a device meant to call for help when a situation had become out of their depth and control. Something about this Psalm reminded me of that rescue device. At the flip of a switch, you can turn on an EPIRB and it will send a signal that connects all the way up to a satellite and then back down to emergency personnel on earth. It is your connection to rescue.

We each have this connection with us at all times because God is

"As we begin to seek God, He responds."

in us. A loving Father in heaven, Jesus living inside our hearts, and the Holy Spirit are our direct access to rescue in times of trouble. As we begin to seek God, He responds. When we pray and ask Him for help, He is faithful to come through. He puts in place the people and things that He has decided to use for our good and His glory and He responds to our call for help whenever we cry out to Him. As testimony after testimony build upon themselves, we begin to say to others, like David did, "May the Lord answer you in the day of trouble." Because we know what it's like to be rescued. We pray that He would protect and send help from His holy sanctuary.

If you think back across your life, have you brought praise to God as a sacrifice in seasons of trouble? Were there moments when you could hardly gather the strength to get out of bed and go to the house of the Lord to praise Him? Or when hurt filled your heart so consuming that you had to tell your soul to bless the Lord because He is worthy? When you didn't understand what God was doing or where He was, but you chose to trust in the name of the Lord your God even in the middle of the battle? These are moments when offering our praise as a sacrifice was hard, painful even, and it cost us. We don't offer sacrifices on physical altars anymore, but our bodies are a sacrifice.

"I appeal to you therefore, brothers, by the mercies of God, to present your bodies as a living sacrifice, holy and acceptable to God, which is your spiritual worship. Do not be conformed to this world, but be transformed by the renewal of your mind, that by testing you may discern what is the will of God, what is good and acceptable and perfect."
Romans 12:1-2 ESV

In seasons of trouble, it would be so easy to retreat and shut down our living sacrifice. It would be easier to quiet the trust we offer to God, when we can't see the end of the story yet. But we must say to our own soul - awake! We have in us the faith to believe that He will be faithful as He has always been while we live in the tension and wait for heaven and home. We must be longing for the day we come face to face with our Savior, and yet be fully alive here on the earth with a passion to share the gospel of Jesus.

There is beauty in the sacrifice for us as believers. We are receivers of the sacrifice Jesus made and that is what Lord remembers of us - what Jesus did for us. We don't have to earn His protection by sacrifice, waiting and hoping in vain. We are covered by the blood of the son of God, who loved us and gave himself for us, and our protection is because of Him. He was and is the perfect sacrifice. It is our assurance and it is also the reason that we can continually offer our lives as an act of spiritual worship.

"May the Lord answer you in the day of trouble! May the name of the God of Jacob protect you! May he send you help from the sanctuary and give you support from Zion! May he remember all your offerings and regard with favor your burnt sacrifices! Selah May he grant you your heart's desire and fulfill all your plans! May we shout for joy over your salvation, and in the name of our God set up our banners! May the Lord fulfill all your petitions! Now I know that the Lord saves his anointed; he will answer him from his holy heaven with the saving might of his right hand. Some trust in chariots and some in horses, but we trust in the name of the Lord our God. They collapse and fall, but we rise and stand upright. O Lord, save the king! May he answer us when we call."

Psalm 20 ESV

READ all of Psalm 20

WRITE this down in your own words: "May the Lord answer you in the day of trouble!"

RESPOND and thank God that He is trustworthy. Thank Him for His faithfulness in every season. Thank Him that as we draw close to Him, He draws close to us. Think about how He has rescued you over and over again. Is there an area in your life that you need to surrender and trust Him more? Take a moment to praise Him for all that He has done and will do.

PRAY: God, help me to trust in Your name. Not in my own name, ability, or strength, but in Your name. Thank you that every word you say is true. Thank you that you never leave or forsake me. Thank you that you are near in times of trouble. God, help me to surrender to you today.

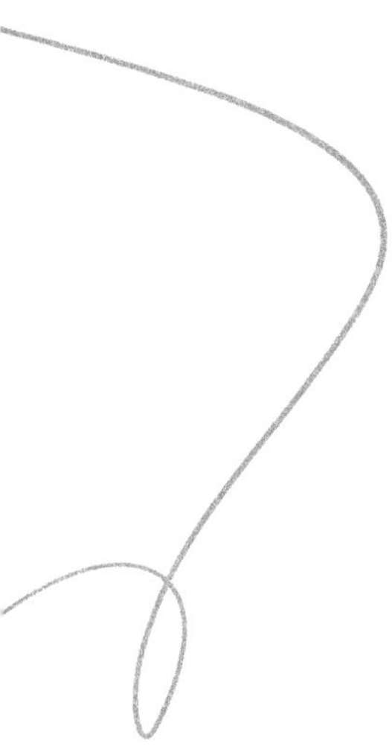

PSALM 20

PSALM 20

"May he grant you your heart's desire and fulfill all your plans! May we shout for joy over your salvation, and in the name of our God set up our banners! May the Lord fulfill all your petitions!"

Psalm 20:4–5 ESV

Can you receive this blessing today?

"May He grant your your heart's desire and fulfill your plans!"

Do you know how we have an assurance of that happening? Obviously, God is not our 'genie in a bottle' and there's not a formula for coaxing what we would like. But here's the secret to never being disappointed. Ask God to make your heart's desires what He desires. Ask Him to make your plans His plans. He gives good gifts to His children because it is His nature. "Every good gift and every perfect gift is from above, coming down from the Father of lights, with whom there is no variation or shadow due to change." (James 1:17 ESV, also see Matthew 7:11 ESV)

"In our knowing, we begin to adjust our plans and purposes to realign with His."

If the answer is "no" from Him, you can trust that it wouldn't be good for you or it wouldn't be good for you right now. My prayer for you today is that your plans would become His plans, your desires His, and that's we would shout in praise for what God has done for us.

"May the Lord fulfill all your petitions!" May he fulfill our prayers and petitions as we trust His plans and purposes. Here's what is so beautiful about trusting God and wanting His plans to be ours. When we choose His way over our own, we can know He will answer our prayers and petitions because we know He is a good Father. We know He gives good gifts and we know that He answers when we call on His name. That means that even when the answer feels long awaited, or when it isn't the answer we hoped for: we know that He is working. In our knowing, we begin to adjust our plans and purposes to realign with His. We get on our knees and say, "God, if this is how you are going to work this all together for my good and your glory, I'm in. Align me to your will and heart, Lord. Let this by my living sacrifice, I lay down my own will and surrender to yours."

"May the Lord answer you in the day of trouble! May the name of the God of Jacob protect you! May he send you help from the sanctuary and give you support from Zion! May he remember all your offerings and regard with favor your burnt sacrifices! Selah May he grant you your heart's desire and fulfill all your plans! May we shout for joy over your salvation, and in the name of our God set up our banners! May the Lord fulfill all your petitions! Now I know that the Lord saves his anointed; he will answer him from his holy heaven with the saving might of his right hand. Some trust in chariots and some in horses, but we trust in the name of the Lord our God. They collapse and fall, but we rise and stand upright. O Lord, save the king! May he answer us when we call."

Psalm 20 ESV

READ all of Psalm 20

WRITE this in your own words: "May we shout for joy over your salvation, and in the name of our God set up our banners! May the Lord fulfill all your petitions!"

RESPOND and thank God that His plans and ways are perfect. Thank Him for His character that is steadfast and unwavering. Thank Him that He is good. Have you been disappointed? Maybe something didn't turn out how you thought it would or you thought you would have received that blessing by now. Ask God to deal with your hurt and disappointment right now. Surrender what you think for what He says.

PRAY God, thank you that you have a perfect plan for my life. Even when I can't see it or feel it, thank you that you are working things together for my good. Heal my disappointment. Make your ways the desire of my heart. I choose you.

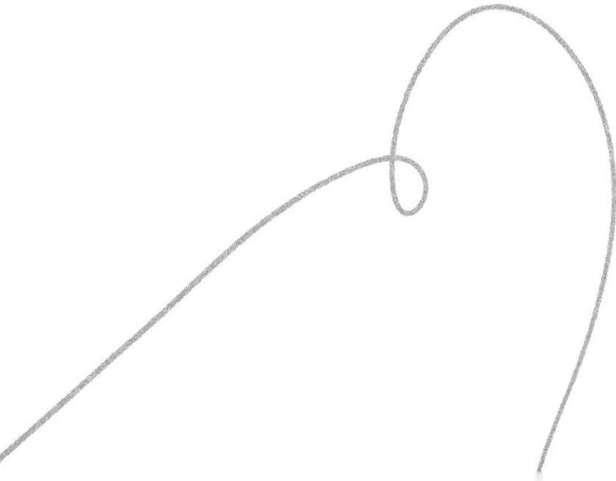

PSALM 20

PSALM 20

THREE

"Now I know that the Lord saves his anointed;
he will answer him from his holy heaven with
the saving might of his right hand. Some trust in
chariots and some in horses, but we trust in the
name of the Lord our God. They collapse and fall,
but we rise and stand upright. O Lord, save the king!
May he answer us when we call."

Psalm 20:6-9 ESV

Now I know. I love this statement. Now I know suggests that because of ________, NOW I know. I have seen God's faithfulness through every season, His rescue over and over, His love for me has never failed and I'm just going to say today that NOW I KNOW. Do you know that He saves you? As a believer, YOU are His anointed. You have been saved because of Jesus - your confession and faith in Christ have saved you. You are chosen and called to shared the gospel and He has anointed you for the task at hand.

"And it is God who establishes us with you in Christ, and has anointed us, and who has also put his seal on us and given us his Spirit in our hearts as a guarantee." (2 Corinthians 1:21-22 ESV)

Have you received that? Do you see yourself as called by God or do you look at others in positions of leadership as the ones who are called? It's so much easier to be thankful for our salvation and then become consumers of the gospel rather than be the kind of believers that bring the gospel to the world around us knowing that we are called and anointed to do so. I believe one of the greatest revelations the church can carry is being a people fully loved and fully awake to their calling. It is the commandment Jesus gives us in Mark 12:30-31 (NIV). We are commanded to be people walking out the doors of our homes to our everyday lives knowing we are loved and chosen to join the rescue effort by bringing Christ to those around us. By offering our everyday walking around as a living sacrifice.

"So here's what I want you to do, God helping you: Take your everyday, ordinary life–your sleeping, eating, going-to-work, and walking-around life–and place it before God as an offering. Embracing what God does for you is the best thing you can do for him. Don't become so well-adjusted to your culture that you fit

into it without even thinking. Instead, fix your attention on God. You'll be changed from the inside out. Readily recognize what he wants from you, and quickly respond to it. Unlike the culture around you, always dragging you down to its level of immaturity, God brings the best out of you, develops well-formed maturity in you."
Romans 12:1-2 MSG

In our every day walking around, we get to carry the light of the world in our hearts. The hope of the world lives in us. Though we may look around and see people losing hope, we can confidently walk forward with hope inside of us.

"We get to carry the light of the world in our hearts."

Have you ever been in a season of trouble? A season where it seemed like darkness was camping around you and yet you had hope somehow, even though the world was crashing down around you. You had peace where there should be none. This is the miracle of God with us. Some trust in chariots and horses, or in the battle weapons that the world would say are the best and strongest, but we don't need all the right tools when we have the Lord on our side. Think of Gideons army in Judges 6:33-7:15. Read it right now and look at what God can do with what looks like less to the world. We don't play by the rules of the world. We obey God's command and trust in His name. He doesn't just answer us when we call, He comes to our rescue and brings life and salvation. This is our God.

"May the Lord answer you in the day of trouble! May the name of the God of Jacob protect you! May he send you help from the sanctuary and give you support from Zion! May he remember all your offerings and regard with favor your burnt sacrifices! Selah May he grant you your heart's desire and fulfill all your plans! May we shout for joy over your salvation, and in the name of our God set up our banners! May the Lord fulfill all your petitions! Now I know that the Lord saves his anointed; he will answer him from his holy heaven with the saving might of his right hand. Some trust in chariots and some in horses, but we trust in the name of the Lord our God. They collapse and fall, but we rise and stand upright. O Lord, save the king! May he answer us when we call."

Psalm 20 ESV

READ all of Psalm 20.

WRITE this down in your own words: "Some trust in chariots and some in horses, but we trust in the name of the Lord our God. They collapse and fall, but we rise and stand upright."

RESPOND and thank God that He has called you and set you apart. Thank Him for the hope, peace, and light that He provides. Where has God positioned you in this season? Write down the people and places where He has called you to carry His light. Ask God for boldness and opportunities to share His love with others.

PRAY and write out your own prayer today. How has Psalm 20 come alive in your heart and helped you to trust in the name of our Lord? Praise, repent, ask and yield as you talk to your heavenly Father who loves you.

PSALM 20

PSALM 20

We leave you with this blessing:

May God answer you in trouble, protect you in perilous days, help you from the sanctuary of His house. May He remember your living as an act of sacrifice and may goodness and mercy follow you all the days of your life. May He give you the desires of your heart and fulfill your plans as you surrender them at His feet. May you shout for joy as salvation fills the streets and may you rejoice as prayers turn into praises. May you rejoice, for the Lord your God is faithful, trustworthy, righteous, and holy. May you stand upright and be full of thanks for all He is and has done. For this is our God.

Peterson, Eugene H. The Message: The Bible in Contemporary Language. NavPress, 2002.

www.ingramcontent.com/pod-product-compliance
Ingram Content Group UK Ltd.
Pitfield, Milton Keynes, MK11 3LW, UK
UKHW062007290726
14090UKWH00022B/1430

9 798868 981456